SHARK
FRENZY

Bull
Sharks

by Rebecca Pettiford

BELLWETHER MEDIA • MINNEAPOLIS, MN

Blastoff! Readers are carefully developed by literacy experts to build reading stamina and move students toward fluency by combining standards-based content with developmentally appropriate text.

Level 1 provides the most support through repetition of high-frequency words, light text, predictable sentence patterns, and strong visual support.

Level 2 offers early readers a bit more challenge through varied sentences, increased text load, and text-supportive special features.

Level 3 advances early-fluent readers toward fluency through increased text load, less reliance on photos, advancing concepts, longer sentences, and more complex special features.

★ **Blastoff! Universe**

Reading Level

Grade **K**

Grades **1–3**

Grade **4**

This edition first published in 2021 by Bellwether Media, Inc.

No part of this publication may be reproduced in whole or in part without written permission of the publisher. For information regarding permission, write to Bellwether Media, Inc., Attention: Permissions Department, 6012 Blue Circle Drive, Minnetonka, MN 55343.

Library of Congress Cataloging-in-Publication Data

Names: Pettiford, Rebecca, author.
Title: Bull sharks / by Rebecca Pettiford.
Description: Minneapolis, MN : Bellwether Media, 2021. | Series: Blastoff! readers: Shark frenzy | Includes bibliographical references and index. | Audience: Ages 5-8 | Audience: Grades 2-3 | Summary: "Simple text and full-color photography introduce beginning readers to bull sharks. Developed by literacy experts for students in kindergarten through third grade"– Provided by publisher.
Identifiers: LCCN 2020036805 (print) | LCCN 2020036806 (ebook) | ISBN 9781644874387 (library binding) | ISBN 9781648341151 (ebook)
Subjects: LCSH: Bull shark–Juvenile literature.
Classification: LCC QL638.95.C3 P48 2021 (print) | LCC QL638.95.C3 (ebook) | DDC 597.3/4-dc23
LC record available at https://lccn.loc.gov/2020036805
LC ebook record available at https://lccn.loc.gov/2020036806

Editor: Rebecca Sabelko   Designer: Josh Brink

Printed in the United States of America, North Mankato, MN.

Table of Contents

What Are Bull Sharks?

snout

Bull sharks swim in warm, **shallow** ocean waters around the world. They are also found in **estuaries**, rivers, and lakes.

These sharks are named for their bull-like looks. They are **aggressive** sharks with thick bodies and wide **snouts**.

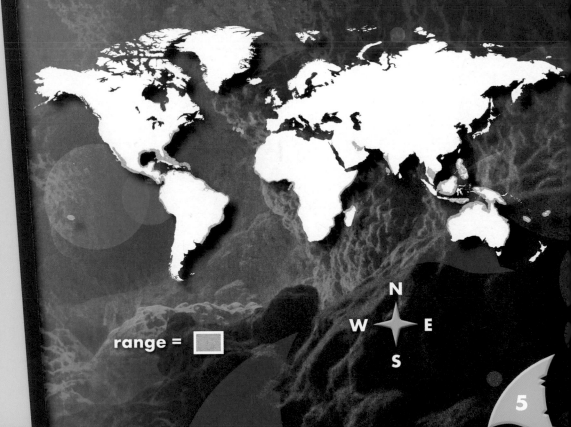

Bull Shark Range

range = ☐

N
W E
S

Bull sharks are **near threatened**. They are fished for their fins, livers, and skin.

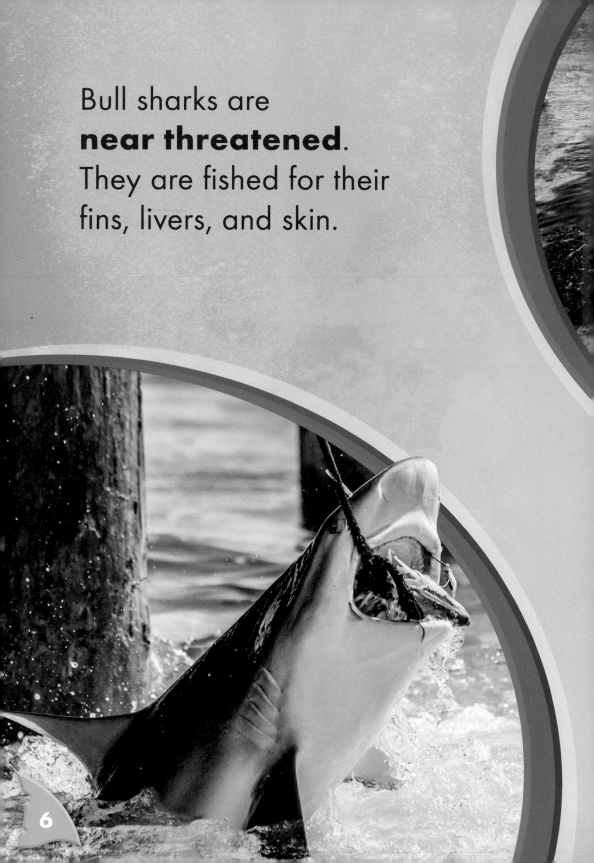

polluted bull shark
habitat

Pollution often fills the coastal waters that bull sharks call home. This human-caused problem damages their **habitat**.

Living in Different Waters

Most sharks cannot live in **freshwater**. They need salt to float.

Bull sharks are **adapted** to freshwater. Special **glands** near their tails help their bodies hold on to salt.

Bull sharks have gray backs and white bellies. This coloring helps them blend in to their **murky** habitat.

Their strong bodies reach up to 11.5 feet (3.5 meters) long.

Shark Sizes

■ average human   ■ bull shark

6 feet (2 meters) long • – ┐

up to 11.5 feet (3.5 meters) long

Bull sharks have small eyes and poor eyesight. They do not need to see well in the cloudy waters they call home.

Identify a Bull Shark

thick body

small eyes

wide snout

They use their excellent sense of smell to find their **prey**.

Water Bullies

Bull sharks are **fierce** hunters. Once they spot food, they ram in to their prey. Then they bite down with their saw-like teeth.

These **predators** have the strongest bite of any shark!

Bull sharks eat bony fish, stingrays, and sea turtles. These **opportunistic feeders** will also eat smaller sharks.

In rivers, bull sharks have been known to eat birds and cows.

Bull Shark Diet

bony fish

stingrays

sea turtles

Bull sharks have their young in estuaries. It keeps their babies safe from ocean predators like tiger sharks.

young bull sharks

From salty seas to rushing rivers,
bull sharks are not afraid
to take charge!

Deep Dive on the Bull Shark

 LIFE SPAN:
up to 32 years

 LENGTH:
up to 11.5 feet (3.5 meters) long

 WEIGHT:
up to 500 pounds (227 kilograms)

 DEPTH RANGE:
0 to 492 feet (0 to 150 meters)

small eyes

wide snout

thick body

Least Concern	Near Threatened	Vulnerable	Endangered	Critically Endangered	Extinct in the Wild	Extinct

conservation status: near threatened

Glossary

adapted—well suited due to changes over a long period of time

aggressive—ready to fight

estuaries—areas where rivers flow into oceans or seas

fierce—strong and intense

freshwater—water that is not salty

glands—body parts that make a substance that the body uses

habitat—land with certain types of plants, animals, and weather

murky—muddy and unclear

near threatened—may become extinct in the near future

opportunistic feeders—animals that eat whatever food is available

pollution—things that make the land, water, or air dirty and unsafe

predators—animals that hunt other animals for food

prey—animals that are hunted by other animals for food

shallow—not deep

snouts—the noses of some animals

To Learn More

AT THE LIBRARY

Nuzzolo, Deborah. *Bull Sharks*. North Mankato, Minn.: Capstone Press, 2018.

Pettiford, Rebecca. *Lemon Sharks*. Minneapolis, Minn.: Bellwether Media, 2021.

Waxman, Laura Hamilton. *Bull Sharks*. Mankato, Minn.: Amicus Ink, 2017.

ON THE WEB

FACTSURFER

Factsurfer.com gives you a safe, fun way to find more information.

1. Go to www.factsurfer.com.

2. Enter "bull sharks" into the search box and click 🔍.

3. Select your book cover to see a list of related content.

Index

The images in this book are reproduced through the courtesy of: Ian Scott, front cover (hero), p. 23; Fiona Ayerst, p. 3; Terry Moore/Stocktrek Images/ Alamy, p. 4; Robby567/ Dreamstime, p. 6; ETrayne04/ Alamy, p. 7; Andrea Izzotti, pp. 8, 20-21; Terry Moore/Stocktrek Images/ Getty, pp. 8-9; Aquarius Traveller, p. 10; chatchai kusolsinchai, p. 12; Allexxandar, p. 13 (ocean floor); Carlos Aguliera, pp. 13, 23; Reinhard Dirscherl/ Alamy, p. 14; Brett Monroe Garner, p. 15; Jun Jacobsen, pp. 16, 19; SunflowerMomma, p. 17 (top left); Eric Carlander, p. 17 (top right); tropicdreams, p. 17 (bottom); justin nuland, p. 18.